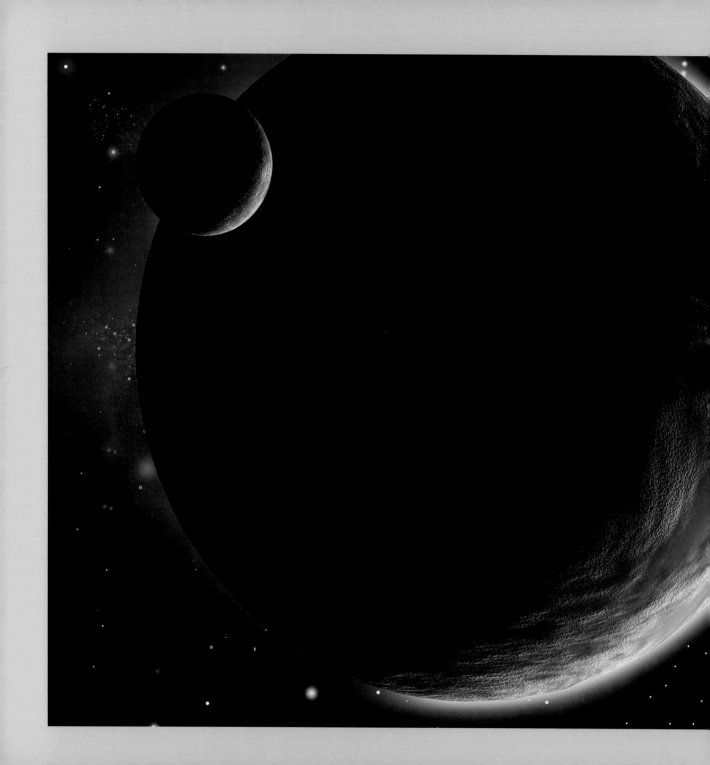

EXPLORE my world

Planets

Becky Baines

NATIONAL
GEOGRAPHIC
KiDS

WASHINGTON, D.C.

Look, it's planet Earth!

From way up high, our planet looks like a floating marble of blue, white, and green. But we know that it's so much more.

Earth has giant oceans and tiny ponds, towering mountains and rolling hilltops.

Warm sunshine.
Fluffy snowflakes.
Stormy showers.
And falling autumn leaves.

Earth has big brown bears and soft cuddly bunnies, mighty lions and bouncy kangaroos. And people, too.

But our planet, Earth, is just one of many planets.

What's a planet?

solar system

A planet travels around a star.

There are billions of stars in our universe. Our star is the sun. The sun holds eight large planets in paths that go round and round.

sun

solar system

You can't see it, but there's a force called gravity that holds the planets in place.

Gravity is also what keeps *you* from floating into space!

Planet Map

The planets that circle our sun make up our solar system. Can you find Earth?

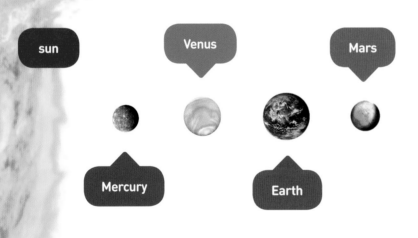

Jupiter

sun

Venus

Mars

Mercury

Earth

Which is your favorite planet? Why?

Can you name all the planets by heart?

Have you ever seen a planet through a telescope?

Start at the sun and count one ... two ... three! Earth is the third planet from the sun.

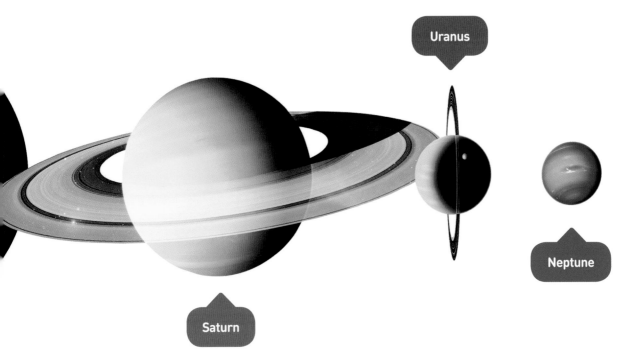

Uranus

Neptune

Saturn

art not to scale

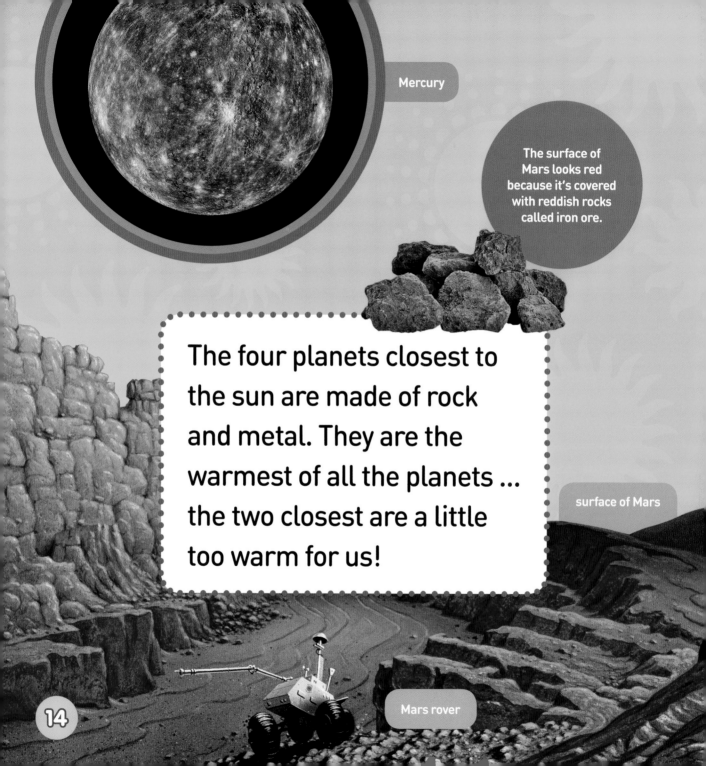

Mercury

The surface of Mars looks red because it's covered with reddish rocks called iron ore.

The four planets closest to the sun are made of rock and metal. They are the warmest of all the planets ... the two closest are a little too warm for us!

surface of Mars

Mars rover

14

Earth is in just the right spot, called the Goldilocks zone. People live where it's not too cold or too hot!

Earth

15

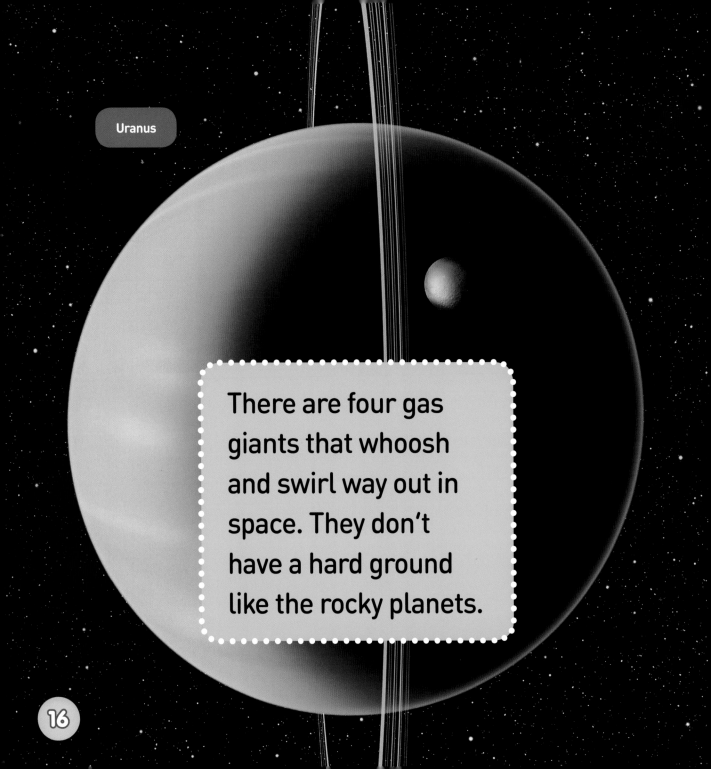

Uranus

There are four gas giants that whoosh and swirl way out in space. They don't have a hard ground like the rocky planets.

Ring Around the Planet

Some planets have rings around them. Saturn's rings are made of dust and ice. Sunlight reflects off the ice and makes the rings sparkle.

Saturn's rings close-up

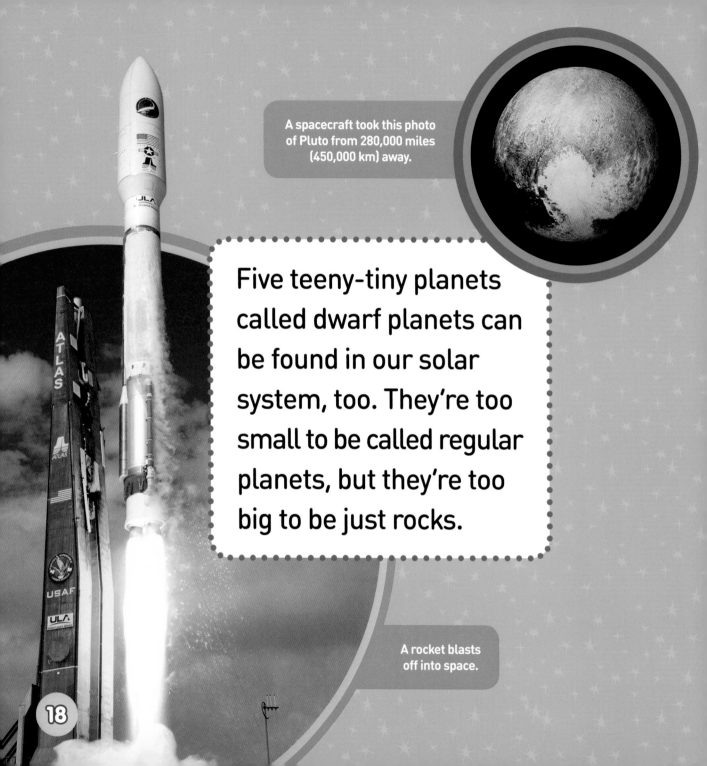

A spacecraft took this photo of Pluto from 280,000 miles (450,000 km) away.

Five teeny-tiny planets called dwarf planets can be found in our solar system, too. They're too small to be called regular planets, but they're too big to be just rocks.

A rocket blasts off into space.

Some dwarf planets are very far away. If you could travel to the farthest one in a rocket, it would take up to 30 years to get there!

Wild Weather!

The weather on other planets is not like here on Earth.

An ordinary day on Venus is 400 times hotter than the hottest summer day on Earth.

surface of Venus

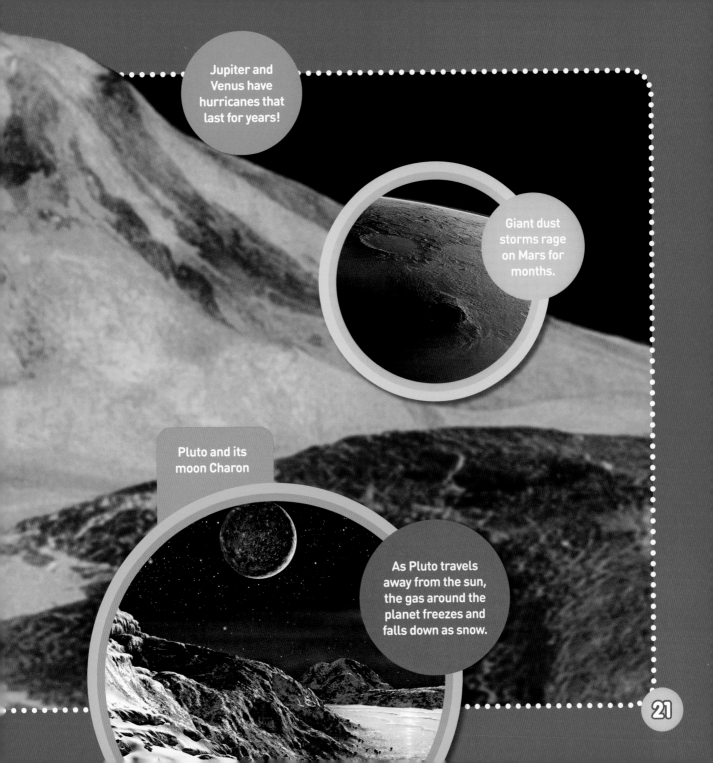

Jupiter and Venus have hurricanes that last for years!

Giant dust storms rage on Mars for months.

Pluto and its moon Charon

As Pluto travels away from the sun, the gas around the planet freezes and falls down as snow.

21

Jupiter and its moons

Some planets have moons. Moons are rocks or ice that circle a planet.

Earth has one moon. But Jupiter has more than 60!

22

Earth and its moon

It took astronauts in a spaceship three days to reach our moon. It would take more than a year to fly from Earth to Jupiter's moons.

Our solar system might seem like a very big place, but it's just one solar system in a galaxy called the Milky Way. So far, scientists have counted 500 other solar systems in our galaxy.

Milky Way galaxy

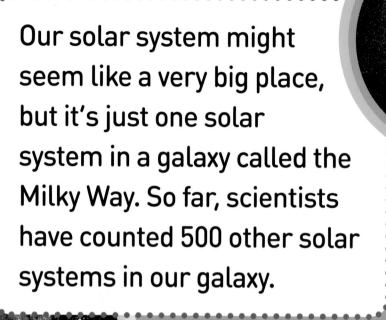

Pinwheel galaxy

Cigar galaxy

The Milky Way is just one of hundreds of billions of galaxies in the universe! If you started counting now, it would take you 30 years to count to just one billion.

Howdy, neighbor!

With so many planets, you might wonder if there are other people or animals out in space. Astronomers are space scientists who wonder the same thing.

The Kepler spacecraft helps scientists on Earth explore space.

Astronomers use telescopes to explore the night sky. They use computers to help them search for planets that are the most like Earth. They have already found a few!

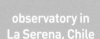

observatory in La Serena, Chile

Look up!

Maybe one day when you're all grown up, you will be able to board a rocket to Mars! Until then, look up at the night sky, watch, wonder, and imagine what else is out there.

Build an Alien

If astronomers did find life on other planets, what do you think those aliens would look like? Would they have ...

spider eyes? ————
duck feet? ————
an elephant trunk?
moose antlers? ————
a dolphin tail?

Grab a piece of paper and draw your own alien!

hello

For sweet Eva
—BB

National Geographic supports K–12 educators with
ELA Common Core Resources. Visit www.natgeoed.org/
commoncore for more information.

The publisher gratefully acknowledges Dr. Brendan Mullan, director
of science for the Wrinkled Brain Project and National Geographic
emerging explorer, for his expert review of the book.

Staff for This Book
Catherine Hughes, *Executive Editor, Preschool Content*
Callie Broaddus, *Art Director* and *Designer*
Christina Ascani, *Photo Editor*
Paige Towler, *Editorial Assistant*
Sanjida Rashid and Rachel Kenny, *Design Production Assistants*
Tammi Colleary-Loach, *Rights Clearance Manager*
Michael Cassady and Mari Robinson, *Rights Clearance Specialists*
Grace Hill, *Managing Editor*
Alix Inchausti, *Production Editor*
Lewis R. Bassford, *Production Manager*
George Bounelis, *Manager, Production Services*
Susan Borke, *Legal and Business Affairs*

ILLUSTRATIONS CREDITS
Cover, David Aguilar; back cover, Johan Swanepoel/Shutterstock; 1,
Steven Puetzer/Getty Images; 2-3, Marc Ward/Stocktrek Images/
Getty Images; 4-5, dem10/Getty Images; 6, Kjell Suwardi Linder/Getty
Images; 7 (UP RT), Stephen Krasemann/Getty Images; 7 (LO LE), anuchit
kamsongmueang/Getty Images; 7 (LO RT), Westend61-FotoFealing/Getty
Images; 8 (UP), Mark Newman/Getty Images; 8 (LO), Callie Broaddus;
8-9, Boris Diaw; 10, Andrzej Wojcicki/Science Photo Library; 11 (UP),
Henning Dalhoff/Science Source; 11 (LO), Jose Antonio Peoas/Science
Source; 12 (LE), Henning Dalhoff/Science Source; 12 (CTR LE), David
Aguilar; 12 (CTR), David Aguilar; 12 (CTR RT), David Aguilar; 12 (RT),
David Aguilar; 12-13 (CTR), David Aguilar; 13 (LE), David Aguilar; 13
(CTR), David Aguilar; 13 (RT), David Aguilar; 14 (BACKGROUND), David A.
Hardy/Science Photo Library; 14 (UP LE), NASA; 14 (CTR), Levent Konuk/
Shutterstock; 15, Detlev van Ravensway/Science Source; 16, David
Aguilar; 17 (BACKGROUND), Brand X/Getty Images; 17 (UP RT), David
Aguilar; 17 (LO LE), Peter Bull Dorling Kindersley/Getty Images; 18 (LE),
NASA; 18 (UP RT), NASA/JHUAPL/SwRI; 19, janez volmajer/Shutter-
stock; 20-21 (BACKGROUND), Science Source; 20 (LO), William Radcliffe/
Getty Images; 21 (UP), Detlev van Ravensway/Science Source; 21 (LO),
David A. Hardy/Science Photo Library; 22-23, A. Gragera, Latin Stock/
Science Source; 23 (BACKGROUND), Brand X/Getty Images; 23 (UP
RT), Donald E. Carroll/Getty Images; 23 (CTR), NASA; 24 (UP RT), Photo
Researchers/Getty Images; 24 (LO LE), European Southern Observatory/
Science Source; 24 (LO), UniqueLight/Shutterstock; 25, NASA; 26, Kauko
Helavuo/Getty Images; 27 (UP), Lynette Cook/Science Source; 27 (LO),
Roger Ressmeyer with Ian Shelton/Corbis; 28-29, Christophe Lehenaff/
Getty Images; 30 (UP), Manoj Shah/Getty Images; 30 (LO), DmitriMaruta/
Shutterstock; 30-31 (LO), Kaya Affan Dengel; 31 (UP RT), Raquel Lonas/
Getty Images; 31 (UP LE), Mark Moffett/Getty Images; 31 (LO LE), Lukas
Gojda/Shutterstock; 31 (LO RT), Patrick Endres/Design Pics/Getty
Images; 32, John Hook/Getty Images

Library of Congress Cataloging-in-Publication Data
Baines, Rebecca, author.
Planets / by Becky Baines.
   pages cm. — (Explore my world)
Audience: Ages 3-7.
ISBN 978-1-4263-2322-5 (pbk. : alk. paper) — ISBN 978-1-4263-2323-2
(library binding : alk. paper)
1. Planets—Juvenile literature. 2. Solar system—Juvenile literature.
I. National Geographic Society (U.S.) II. Title. III. Series: Explore my world.
QB602.B345 2016
523.2--dc23
2015027843

Printed in the United States of America
17/WOR/2